60 Days Of Questions
For Couples

Copyright © 2020 by Blue Rock Couple Workbooks

All rights reserved. This book or any portion thereof may not be reproduced or used in any manner whatsoever without the express written permission of the publisher except for the use of brief quotations in a book review.

Printed in the United States of America

How to use this book:

Everyone knows that being a couple, married or not, takes work. That's why this workbook is designed to start conversations and get to know each other well.

There is a mixture of non sexual conversational items on the list, as well as sexual. Every healthy relationship has a healthy intimacy in and out of the bedroom.

This can be done 60 consecutive days, you can do every other day, or whatever works for you.

Each day there is a conversation starter, write down your reaction in a notepad for review. This forces the conversation and activity being done! If this is e-book version, simply discuss each question.

A good practice would be to do this at bedtime every night.

Let's begin!

Day 1

Besides on the lips, where do you like to be kissed?

How often do you like to be kissed?

Her Reaction

____

____

____

____

____

____

His Reaction

____

____

____

____

____

____

____

Day 2

What kind of music gets you in the mood?

Share specific types or artists and songs.

Her Reaction

His Reaction

Day 3

Which physical
parts of my body
do you like best?

What about
favorite body parts
of yours?

Her Reaction

His Reaction

Day 4

What's your
favorite sex
position?

Which one do you
not like as much?

Her Reaction

His Reaction

Day 5

What's your
favorite gadget that
you can't live
without?

Her Reaction

His Reaction

Day 6

Strip Clubs; are
they hot to go to as
a couple or trashy?

Her Reaction

His Reaction

Day 7

If given a hall pass for a celebrity, who would you want to have sex with?

Her Reaction

His Reaction

Day 8

Where in public would you like to have sex at sometime?

Her Reaction

His Reaction

Day 9

What's an adult beverage that you like that I may not know about?

Her Reaction

____

____

____

____

____

____

____

His Reaction

____

____

____

____

____

____

____

Day 10

If we were to roleplay, who would you be?

Who should I be?

Her Reaction

His Reaction

Day 11

Sex in a hot tub or
sex in a shower?

Her Reaction

____

____

____

____

____

____

____

His Reaction

____

____

____

____

____

____

____

____

Day 12

Would you ever do strip poker or similar game in a group setting?

Her Reaction

____

____

____

____

____

____

____

His Reaction

____

____

____

____

____

____

____

Day 13

Do you like taking nude pictures?

What about sex videos?

Would you ever?

Her Reaction

His Reaction

Day 14

Do you like dirty talk?

Or

Pillow talk after sex?

Her Reaction

His Reaction

Day 15

Sleep in the nude
or go to bed with
pajamas on?

Her Reaction

His Reaction

Day 16

Would you have sex somewhere that you might get caught?

Her Reaction

His Reaction

Day 17

What does your
ideal vacation look
like?

Her Reaction

His Reaction

Day 18

Discuss any
childhood
memories that are
very clear or vivid
in your mind that
you love.

Her Reaction

His Reaction

Day 19

Ideally, how many times per week would you like to have sex together?

Her Reaction

His Reaction

Day 20

What are you most proud of in your life?

Any disappointments?

Her Reaction

His Reaction

Day 21

Would you rather be the most attractive person in the world or funniest person in the world?

Her Reaction

His Reaction

Day 22

Do you like being
massaged?

Do you like
sensual
massages?

Her Reaction

His Reaction

Day 23

What would be a
good erotic date?

Her Reaction

____

____

____

____

____

____

____

His Reaction

____

____

____

____

____

____

____

Day 24

Sex at bedtime or sex in the morning?

Her Reaction

His Reaction

Day 25

Do you like giving oral sex a lot?

Do you like receiving oral sex? How do you like it?

Her Reaction

His Reaction

Day 26

Have you ever
watched a couple
have sex?

Would you?

Her Reaction

His Reaction

Day 27

Would you ever be
fine with being tied
up in bed?

Her Reaction

His Reaction

Day 28

Sex in the car?

Her Reaction

His Reaction

Day 29

What is your ideal
retirement?

Where would you
want to live?

Her Reaction

____

____

____

____

____

____

His Reaction

____

____

____

____

____

____

Day 30

Do you like to send and receive dirty and flirty text messages?

Her Reaction

____

His Reaction

Day 31

Rough and passionate sex or slow love making?

Her Reaction

____

____

____

____

____

____

His Reaction

____

____

____

____

____

____

Day 32

Would you have sex while another couple is also in the room?

Her Reaction

His Reaction

Day 33

What is the career you would love to have if it's not your current one?

Her Reaction

His Reaction

Day 34

What's totally
off-limits in bed?

What would you
like to try?

Her Reaction

His Reaction

Day 35

What's the most adventurous thing you've ever done, sexuallly or non sexual?

Her Reaction

His Reaction

Day 36

What's the ideal
date night in your
opinion?

Her Reaction

____

____

____

____

____

____

____

His Reaction

____

____

____

____

____

____

____

Day 37

If you can only eat one food for the rest of your life, what would it be?

Her Reaction

____

____

____

____

____

____

____

His Reaction

____

____

____

____

____

____

____

Day 38

Which would you
rather wear?

Brief style panties
or thongs?

Her Reaction

His Reaction

Day 39

Would you ever have sex at work if you can get away with it?

Her Reaction

His Reaction

Day 40

What's your favorite outfit to wear for me?

Which outfit of mine do you like best?

Her Reaction

____

____

____

____

____

____

____

His Reaction

____

____

____

____

____

____

____

Day 41

What's your favorite series of all time to binge watch?

Her Reaction

His Reaction

Day 42

On a guy, what do
you like better?
Chest or butt?

On a girl, what do
you like better?
Breasts or butt?

Her Reaction

His Reaction

Day 43

Rather stay at a resort or take a cruise?

Her Reaction

His Reaction

Day 44

Which do you like better, dogs or cats?

Her Reaction

His Reaction

Day 45

Who is your
favorite superhero?

Her Reaction

His Reaction

Day 46

When performing 69, man on top or woman on top?

Her Reaction

His Reaction

Day 47

Are you in the mile high club? Would you ever join the mile high club?

Her Reaction

____

____

____

____

____

____

____

His Reaction

____

____

____

____

____

____

____

Day 48

Describe your
perfect Wedding
Day.

Her Reaction

____

____

____

____

____

____

____

____

His Reaction

____

____

____

____

____

____

____

____

Day 49

Women: Spit or swallow?

Men: Lick or suck

Her Reaction

____

____

____

____

____

____

His Reaction

____

____

____

____

____

____

____

Day 50

What's your
favorite gifts to
receive?

Her Reaction

His Reaction

Day 51

What's your favorite place to visit?

Her Reaction

His Reaction

Day 52

What's one talent
you wish you can
have?

Her Reaction

____

____

____

____

____

____

____

His Reaction

____

____

____

____

____

____

____

Day 53

Would you ever have a "Naked Day"?

Hang out all day naked in the house.

Her Reaction

His Reaction

Day 54

What's one movie you can watch over and over again?

Her Reaction

His Reaction

Day 55

Would you ever do anything risky in a movie theater?

Her Reaction

His Reaction

Day 56

Sunbathing nude;
sexy or not?

What about nude
swimming?

Her Reaction

His Reaction

Day 57

If you won the lottery tomorrow, what would you do with the money?

Her Reaction

____

____

____

____

____

____

____

His Reaction

____

____

____

____

____

____

____

____

Day 58

Going out in public
with a dress/skirt
and no panties.

Hot or not?

Her Reaction

His Reaction

Day 59

Public displays of affection in public is something you like or don't like?

Her Reaction

His Reaction

Day 60

Would you ever be naked or flash in public?

Her Reaction

His Reaction

www.ingramcontent.com/pod-product-compliance
Lightning Source LLC
Chambersburg PA
CBHW071528150726
48000CB00002B/728